Political Changes

THE ADMINISTRATIONS OF NIXON, FORD AND CARTER

Government Book Grade 7 |
Children's Government Books

BABY PROFESSOR
EDUCATION KIDS

First Edition, 2022

Published in the United States by Speedy Publishing LLC, 40 E Main Street, Newark, Delaware 19711 USA.

© 2022 Baby Professor Books, an imprint of Speedy Publishing LLC

Baby Professor Books are available at special discounts when purchased in bulk for industrial and sales-promotional use. For details contact our Special Sales Team at Speedy Publishing LLC, 40 E Main Street, Newark, Delaware 19711 USA. Telephone (888) 248-4521 Fax: (210) 519-4043.

10 9 8 7 6 * 5 4 3 2 1

Print Edition: 9781541958821
Digital Edition: 9781541961821
Hardcover Edition: 9781541996786

See the world in pictures. Build your knowledge in style.
www.speedypublishing.com

Table of Contents

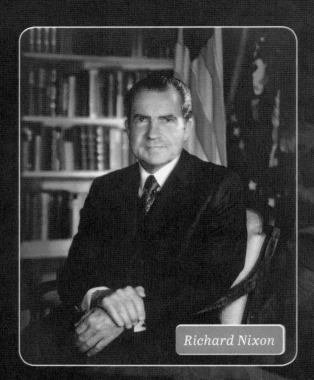

Richard Nixon

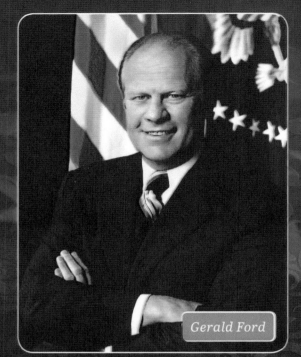

Gerald Ford

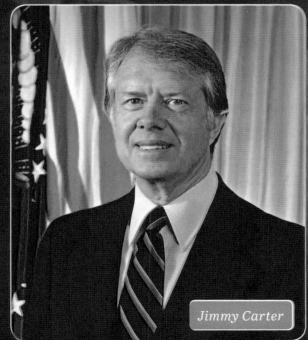

Jimmy Carter

The United States saw many political changes from 1969 to 1981. During this period, three different men served as the President of the United States. The first chapter will discuss some aspects of the administration of Richard Nixon. The second chapter will discuss some aspects of the administration of Gerald Ford. The third chapter will discuss some aspects of the administration of Jimmy Carter.

Richard Nixon

Chapter One:
The Administration of Richard Nixon

Richard M. Nixon was the President of the United States from 1969 to 1974. He won the presidential election by a narrow margin over Hubert H. Humphrey.

Hubert H. Humphrey

Richard Nixon

9

When Nixon became president, the economy was weak, and the federal government had very little money.

Some of Nixon's Domestic Actions and Policies:

The economy was weak, and the federal government had very little money when Nixon became president. To reduce the inflation rate, Nixon tried to have interest rates increased. This was in an attempt to dissuade people from taking out loans. Nixon did not raise the amount of money that the government would spend. He froze wages and prices for ninety days.

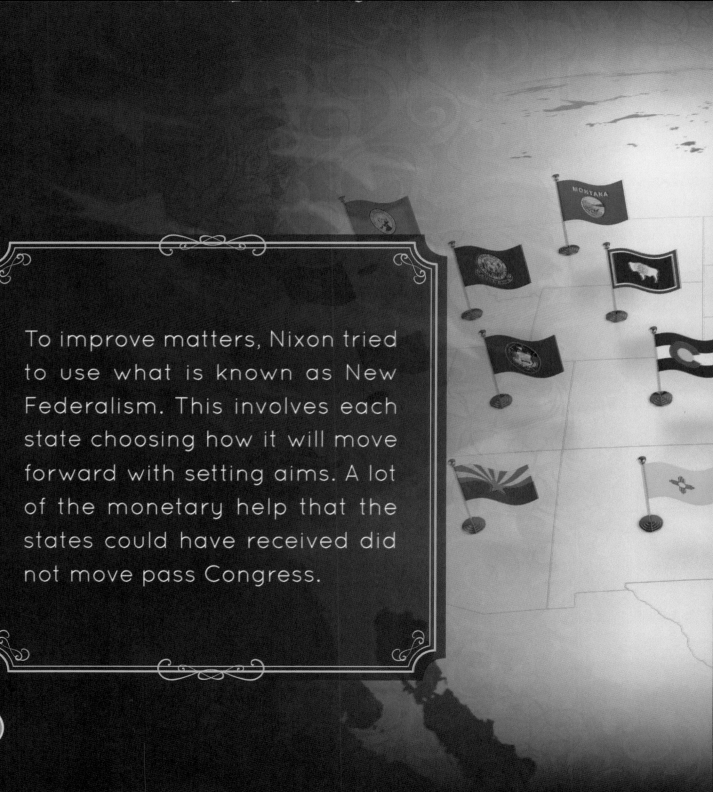

To improve matters, Nixon tried to use what is known as New Federalism. This involves each state choosing how it will move forward with setting aims. A lot of the monetary help that the states could have received did not move pass Congress.

New Federalism involves each state choosing how it will move forward with setting aims.

GOVERNMENT AID

Nixon wanted to make reforms in the welfare system. This is the system which provides financial assistance to the poor and needy. He came up with a concept known as a *negative income tax*. It was supposed to motivate people to find work themselves so that they would not have to rely on government handouts. It would allow those who did not earn a certain amount of money to receive a stipend or pay. It would be done in a way that motivated them to become self sufficient. This plan did not succeed.

Nixon also attempted to have racial desegregation. This, too, was not successful. He did manage to be the first American president to implement affirmative action. He required contractors who worked for the government to provide jobs to a certain number of minorities.

Nixon did manage to be the first American president to implement affirmative action.

Nixon required contractors who worked for the government to provide jobs to a certain number of minorities.

Some of Nixon's Foreign Actions and Policies:

Leonid Brezhnev

Nixon did several things to try to make relations better between the United States and the Soviet Union. One thing is that he traveled to the Soviet Union. While in Moscow, he and the Soviet leader, Leonid Brezhnev, signed an agreement.

It said that both countries would only produce and hold a certain number of nuclear missiles and warheads. This agreement was known as SALT.

Another thing that Nixon did was that he let the Soviets purchase grain from the United States at an incredibly low price. The Soviet Union ended up receiving grain that would normally have been sold for a billion dollars for much less!

Nixon let the Soviets purchase grain from the United States at an incredibly low price.

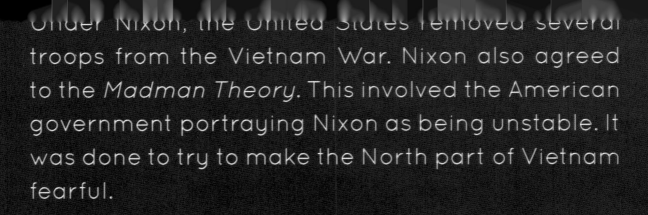

Under Nixon, the United States removed several troops from the Vietnam War. Nixon also agreed to the *Madman Theory*. This involved the American government portraying Nixon as being unstable. It was done to try to make the North part of Vietnam fearful.

American soldiers during the Vietnam War, 1965.

Bombs were dropped over two neighboring countries of Vietnam during Nixon's Administration.

In turn, the American government hoped that it would lead to a ceasefire. Bombs were also dropped over two neighboring countries of Vietnam during Nixon's Administration. One country was Laos. The other was Cambodia. This was called *Operation Menu*.

Nixon with his edited transcripts of the White House tapes subpoenaed by the Special Prosecutor, during his televised speech on Watergate on April 29, 1974.

Nixon and the Watergate Scandal:

Nixon may mostly be remembered for his involvement in the Watergate Scandal. This scandal took place in 1972. Nixon was uncertain about whether he would win a second term as President. His re-election committee came up with different ways of undermining the opposition's campaign. The Watergate Scandal was one of them.

Nixon was a Republican. Five men were hired as spies to gather campaign information from the Democrats. The five ended up breaking into the Watergate Building. This is where the Democrats were headquartered.

Watergate East, part of the Watergate Complex, Foggy Bottom, Washington, D.C.

Accused Men of "Watergate Seven" Walking to Trial. (Left to right): Virgilio Gonzales; Henry Rothblatt, attorney; Bernard Baker; Frank Sturgis; and Eugenio Martinez.

Five men were arrested for the crime. In January of 1973, they were found guilty after going to trial.

Later, an investigative committee was formed to look into the matter. It was discovered that Nixon had told staff members to make it look like the Republicans had nothing to do with the crime. There was evidence that Nixon was responsible for trying to cover up the crime.

House Banking Committee hearing on Watergate Incident.

Nixon announces his resignation as President of the USA in 1974 following the Watergate scandal.

Before he could be impeached, he resigned. To be impeached means a person in public office is being charged with doing something wrong. There were three impeachment charges.

Several charges were investigated by the Senate Committee. One was that there was an attempt to cover up the Watergate Affair. There was a misuse of campaign funds for this purpose. There was an attempt to block the FBI from investigating. Burglars were hired. Phones were tapped illegally. Tape recordings of Nixon's voice were found, showing his involvement in the cover up.

U.S. Senator Howard Baker, left, listens as U.S. Senator Sam Ervin, Chairman of the U.S. Senate Watergate Committee, right, makes a statement during the hearings investigating the Watergate break-in during the Summer of 1973 in Washington, D.C.

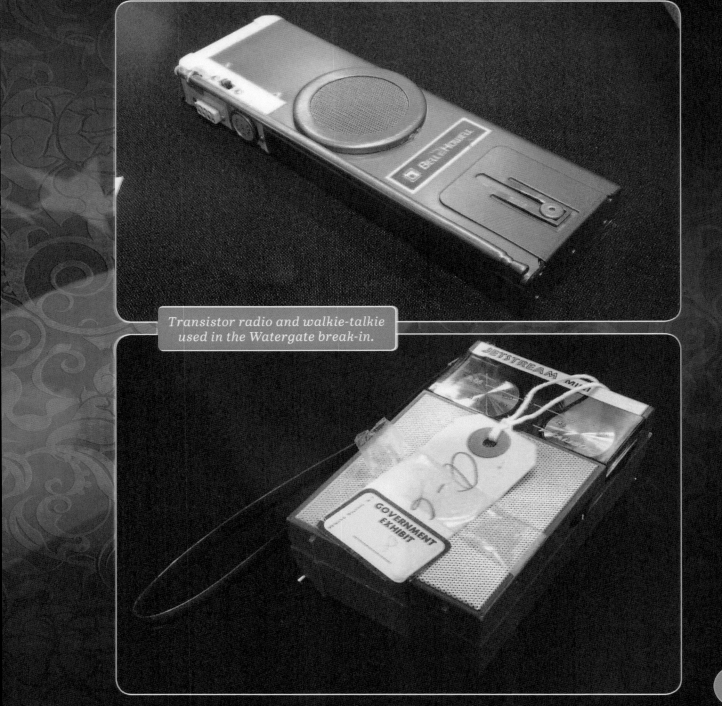

Transistor radio and walkie-talkie used in the Watergate break-in.

Gerald Ford

Chapter Two: The Administration of Gerald Ford

How and When Ford Became President:

Gerald R. Ford became the president of the United States under unique circumstances. He was appointed to the office by the outgoing president, Richard Nixon. As soon as Nixon resigned, Ford took over as the president. This was in 1974. Ford continued in the position until 1977.

The swearing in of President Gerald Ford by Supreme Court Chief Justice Warren Burger.

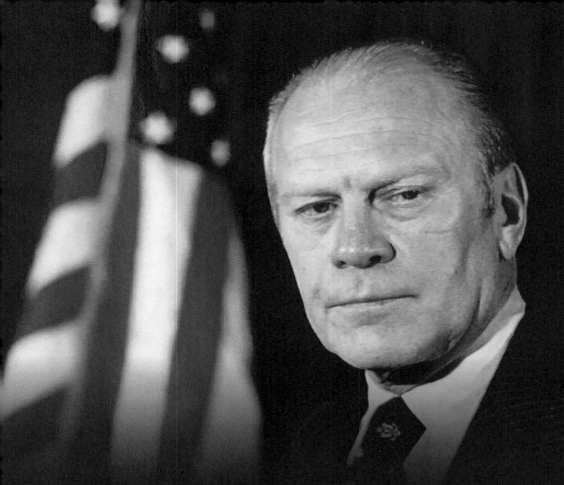

When Ford took the presidential office, things in the United States were uncertain. This was not only because people were leery of the government, but also because the economy was not stable. It was Ford's job to help the American people through this difficult time, and to regain their trust.

35

President Ford signs the Nixon Pardon at The Oval Office, The White House, Washington, D.C. on September 8, 1974.

FORD'S DOMESTIC ACTIONS:
A FULL PARDON:

To help the country move forward, and away from focusing on the Watergate Scandal, Ford decided to grant Nixon a full pardon. A lot of Americans did not appreciate this decision. Many were upset. They did not think that it was just.

A full pardon means that a person is shown grace. He or she does not have to receive any punishment for breaking the law. The person is cleared of all wrongdoing and his or her rights are fully restored.

In addition to granting a pardon to Nixon, Ford also gave pardons to some men who refused to serve in the Vietnam War. This also upset some Americans.

President Ford appearing at the House Judiciary Subcommittee hearing on pardoning former President Richard Nixon, Washington, D.C.

37

THE EQUAL RIGHTS AMENDMENT:

When Ford was president, there was a proposal to amend the Constitution. It was to add that a woman was equal to a man. Although Ford was in favor of the amendment, it never received ratification.

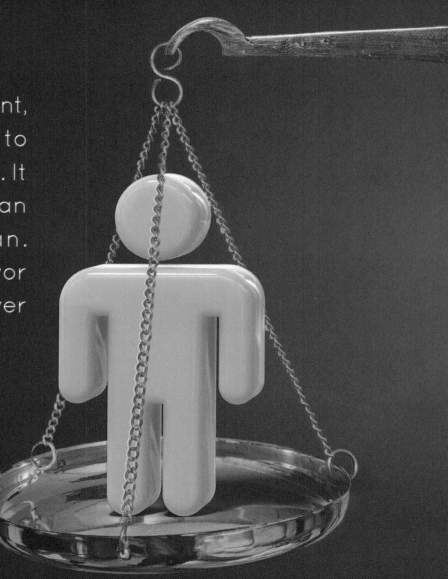

When Ford was president, there was a proposal to amend the Constitution to add that a woman was equal to a man.

Ford tried to tackle unemployment.

A Poor Economy:

Ford decided that lowering the inflation rate would be helpful in improving the economy. He tried to tackle unemployment. He also reduced the tax rate in an attempt to boost economic growth.

At the same time, his advice to the American people was to be careful about not overspending. Ford thought that these actions, together, would control inflation. However, this did not happen.

Ford's advice to the American people was to be careful about not overspending.

Did you know?

The term *stagflation* came about in the decade of the 1970s. It was used to describe an increase in job loss and inflation at the same time. Before that, those who studied Economics did not think that these two issues could happen together. Ford was not keen on finding a solution to this problem by having the government become more involved.

STAGFLATION

RECESSIONARY

GDP **UNEMPLOYMENT** **DEMAND**

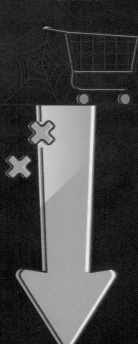

INFLATI

In a stagflation, the unemployment and inflation rates increase while deman and GDP decrease.

FORD'S FOREIGN ACTIONS:

During the Ford Administration, an ally of the United States was attacked. The ally was Israel. It was common for American politicians to support Israel. Ford, on the other hand, would not supply substantial monetary aid to the Israelis.

Official documents from Former President Gerald Ford's administration, dealing with the Israel-Palestine conflict, are kept at the Gerald R. Ford Presidential Library in Ann Arbor, Michigan.

Although Israel was the country that was attacked, Ford felt that its response was aggressive. He threatened to remove important assistance to Israel if the Israelis refused an immediate peaceful resolution to the war.

President Ford meeting with Prime Minister of Israel Yitzhak Rabin, Oval Office, The White House, June 11, 1975.

On August 1, 1975, 35 head of states signed the Helsinki Accords. From left to right: Erich Honecker, East Germany's First Secretary, U.S. President Ford, Austrian Chancellor Bruno Kreisky, Leo Tindemans from Belgium, Todor Zhivkov of Bulgaria, Pierre Trudeau, Canada.

Ford helped to negotiate and sign a treaty with over thirty other nations. It was known as the Helsinki Accords. This agreement had to do with international laws and ideas of what was decent and moral. This was an important agreement because it involved so many European nations. The Soviet Union even signed it. This was a step in helping to make relations better with the two opposing superpowers of the Cold War.

Overall, Ford was not viewed as a popular president. Many saw him as being weak in the role. There were two attempted assassinations on his life in 1975. Ford lost the presidential election the following year to Jimmy Carter.

U.S. Secret Service lead President Ford to safety after an attempted assassination on September 5, 1975 in Sacramento, California.

President Ford escaping a second assasination on September 22, 1975 at San Francisco, California.

Did you know?

Many Middle Eastern Arab countries refused to sell oil to the United States in 1973 due to American aid to the Israelis. The Arab Israeli War began in 1973. It was between several Arab countries and Israel. The Arab countries did not want the United States to help Israel. To retaliate, they put an embargo on oil being exported to the United States.

The United States experienced a fuel shortage during the 1973 oil embargo imposed by Arab oil-producing countries.

Egyptian army crossing into the Sinai from the West Bank of the Nile during the Arab Israeli War in 1973.

Jimmy Carter

Chapter Three: The Administration of Jimmy Carter

Jimmy Carter held the presidential office from 1977 to 1981. His full name was James Earl Carter, Jr. While he was running for the office, he promised to lead the country with strong morals.

Jimmy Carter held the presidential office from 1977 to 1981.

Jimmy Carter Inauguration as the 39th president of the United States, January 20, 1977.

Despite Ford's reputation and the Watergate Scandal still on people's minds, Carter did not win the general election by a wide margin. He only received 50.1 percent of the votes.

President Jimmy Carter delivers the Malaise Speech on July 15, 1979.

SOME OF CARTER'S DOMESTIC POLICIES AND HAPPENINGS:

Like Ford, Carter was the president when the economy was poor. In 1979, he gave a speech to address the issue. It was known as the Malaise Speech.

federal register

MONDAY, JANUARY 24, 1977

PART IX

THE PRESIDENT

Jimmy Carter

■

PRESIDENTIAL PROCLAMATION OF PARDON OF JANUARY 21, 1977

EXECUTIVE ORDER RELATING TO PROCLAMATION OF PARDON

Proclamation 4483 was a presidential proclamation issued by Jimmy Carter in 1977 which granted pardons to those who evaded the draft in the Vietnam War.

To deal with division on the Vietnam War, Carter issued a pardon for anyone who refused to serve during this war. This action received both criticism and praise.

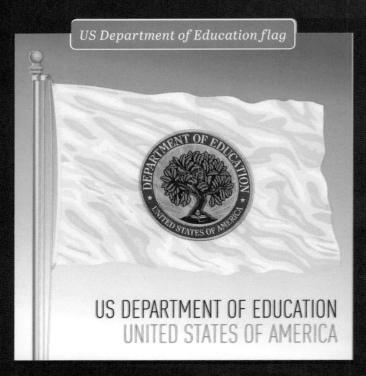

US Department of Education flag

US DEPARTMENT OF EDUCATION
UNITED STATES OF AMERICA

Flag of the United States
Department of Energy

Carter was noted for giving federal jobs to minorities and women. He also decreased taxes.

Two new Cabinet departments were created during Carter's presidency. One was the Department of Education. The other was the Department of Energy.

There was an energy crisis during the Carter Administration. This was because the Middle East lowered the amount of oil it exported. To deal with this issue, Carter rationed gas, developed new types of taxes, proposed developing other energy sources. The US Senate would not accept the latter. They thought that it would not be good for the economy. They also feared that it would only add pressure on businesses.

There was an energy crisis during the Carter Administration because the Middle East lowered the amount of oil it exported.

Jimmy Carter and General Omar Torrijos shake hands after signing the Panama Canal Treaty, September 7, 1977.

SOME OF CARTER'S FOREIGN POLICIES AND HAPPENINGS:

The Torrijos-Carter Treaty was signed during Carter's presidency. By signing it, the United States was giving up its control of the Panama Canal. Panama would control the canal. Although the agreement was signed in 1977, it was not

The United States and the Soviet Union agreed to restrict the number of nuclear weapons that each country made. Carter signed this agreement with the Soviets. It was known as the SALT II Treaty.

Jimmy Carter and Leonid Brezhnev signing the SALT II treaty, June 18, 1979, at the Hofburg Palace, in Vienna, Austria.

Carter played a role in the Camp David Accords. These accords were several meetings as well as peace agreements between Egypt and Israel. They helped to shape Middle East politics for many years.

Egyptian President Anwar El Sadat, Jimmy Carter and Israeli Prime Minister Menachem Begin at the Camp David Accords Signing Ceremony.

Carter was known for his support of human rights as well as democratic views. Both these views contributed to his decision to boycott the Summer Olympics in Moscow in 1980. It was in response to the Soviet Union invading Afghanistan.

On New Year's Day in 1979, the United States and China agreed to have complete diplomatic relations with each other. Carter played a role in this agreement.

Chinese Vice Premier Deng Xiaoping applauds as US President Jimmy Carter stands behind a podium at the White House, Washington, D.C., January 1979.

In November 1979, over fifty people were held hostage in the American Embassy in Iran. It became known as the Iran Hostage Crisis. It happened during a revolution there. Many people did not think that Carter handled the situation well. Most of the people remained in hostage until January 1981.

Two American hostages in the Iran hostage crisis.

President Carter announces new sanctions against Iran in retaliation for taking U.S. hostages.

DID YOU KNOW?

After leaving the presidency, Carter did many other things. Along with his wife, he established the Carter Center. This is for the promotion of peace and upholding human rights. The center is in Atlanta, Georgia. He assisted in building houses for the needy with Habitat for Humanity. He was awarded the Nobel Peace Prize in 2002.

Rosalynn Carter, wife of US president Jimmy Carter

Jimmy Carter and his wife Rosalynn help build homes for Habitat for Humanity in Edmonton Alta.

Nobel Peace Prize 2002 given to President Jimmy Carter on display at Jimmy Carter Presidential Library & Museum, Carter Center, Atlanta, Georgia.

Summary

From 1969 to 1981, the United States saw political changes. There were three different presidents during this time period. One was Richard Nixon. He tried to help the economy. He also managed to implement an affirmative action program. He helped to make relations a bit smoother with the Soviet Union. Nixon ended up resigning before he could be impeached. This was for his role in the Watergate Scandal.

Gerald Ford was appointed to the role of presidency after Nixon resigned. Ford was generally not viewed as being a strong president. He did not win re-election. Following Ford, Jimmy Carter served as the president of the United States. He was known for making some positive progress in foreign affairs. However, many were displeased with how he handled the Iran Hostage Crisis.

Printed in Great Britain
by Amazon

25554977R00043